KU-244-301

SCIENCE
in Action
THE HUMAN BODY

YOUR
HEART AND
LUNGS

Sally Hewitt

Publisher: Maxime Boucknooghe
Editorial Director: Victoria Garrard
Art Director: Miranda Snow
Series Editor: Claudia Martin
Series Designer: Bruce Marshall
Photographer: Michael Wicks
Illustrator: Chris Davidson
Consultant: Kristina Routh

Copyright © QED Publishing 2016

First published in the UK in 2016 by
QED Publishing
Part of The Quarto Group
The Old Brewery, 6 Blundell Street,
London, N7 9BH

All rights reserved. No part of this publication may be
reproduced, stored in a retrieval system, or transmitted
in any form or by any means, electronic, mechanical,
photocopying, recording or otherwise, without the prior
permission of the publisher, nor be otherwise circulated
in any form of binding or cover other than that in which
it is published and without a similar condition being
imposed on the subsequent purchaser.

A catalogue record for this book is available
from the British Library.

ISBN 978 1 78493 461 3

Printed in China

Picture credits

t = top, b = bottom, c = centre, l = left, r = right,
fc = front cover

Alamy 4 Digital Vision, 11 Bubbles Photolibrary
Corbis 14 Daniel Attia/Zefa, 18 Jim Craigmyle
Getty Images 13 Stephen Frink, 16 Kevin Mackintosh
Science Photo Library 10 Mauro Fermariello
Shutterstock fc Gregory Johnston, 4l Z Adam, 5t Gelpi,
5b Jaimie Duplass, 6 Hayati Kayhan, 8b Supri Suharjoto,
9 Darren Baker, 15 Juriah Mosim, 17t Julian Rovagnati,
17b Arvind Balarama, 19t Thomas M Perkins, 19b Vadim
Ponomarenko, 20 Olga Lyubkina/StudioNewmarket, 21l
Hallgerd, 21r Yvan Dube

Words in **bold** can be
found in the glossary
on page 22.

DUDLEY SCHOOLS LIBRARY SERVICE	
S00000787572	
£10.99	J612.1
09-Jun-2016	PETERS

Contents

Your amazing heart 4

Heart beat 6

Veins and arteries 8

Blood 10

Lungs 12

Breathe in... 14

Breathe out... 16

Talking 18

Healthy heart and lungs 20

Glossary 22

Index 23

Next steps 24

Your amazing heart

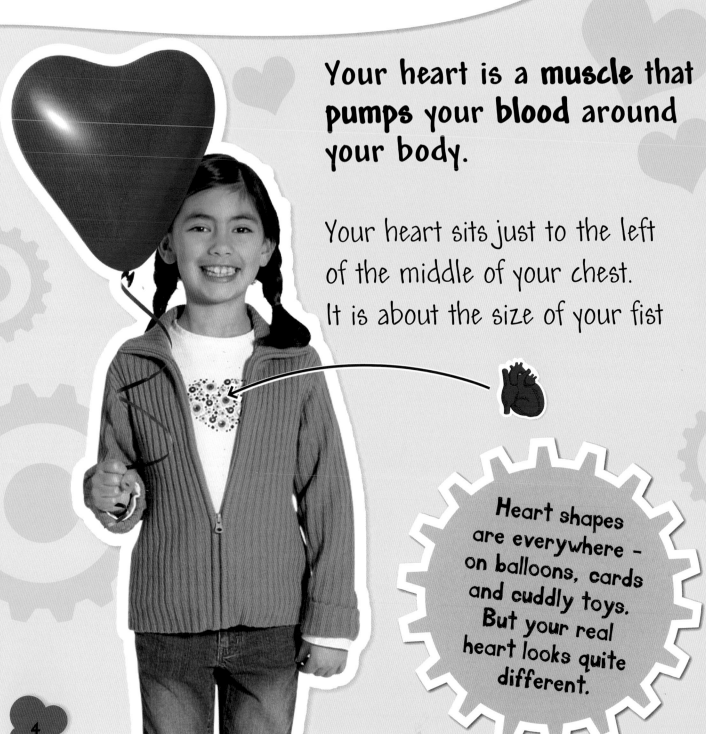

Your heart is a **muscle** that **pumps** your **blood** around your body.

Your heart sits just to the left of the middle of your chest. It is about the size of your fist

Heart shapes are everywhere – on balloons, cards and cuddly toys. But your real heart looks quite different.

A doctor listens to your heart pumping in your chest using a stethoscope.

Your heart is always working. It pumps blood all day and night to all the different parts of your body. Every part of your body – your brain, **lungs**, skin etc – needs blood to keep it working properly.

Your heart doesn't need to work as hard when you are asleep. It has to beat faster when you wake up and start moving.

Heart beat

Your heart muscle squeezes over and over again giving a heart 'beat'.

When your heart fills up with blood, the heart muscle squeezes to push this blood out into your **blood vessels**. Your heart then fills up with more blood.

Activity

When you're next in the bath, try filling a rubber duck, squeezy bath toy or even a plastic bottle with water, then squeezing it out. Do it again... and again! This is like your heart muscles squeezing as it pumps blood.

Be careful where you squirt the water!

Each side of your heart has two rooms or 'chambers'.
The right side of your heart pumps blood into your lungs
to collect **oxygen**. The left side pumps this blood back into
your body.

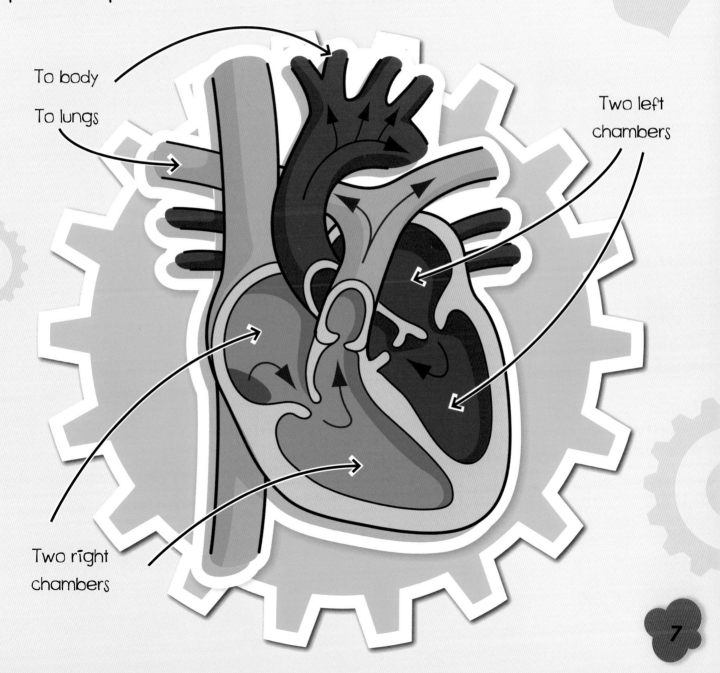

To body

To lungs

Two left
chambers

Two right
chambers

Veins and arteries

Arteries
(red)

Veins
(blue)

Your heart pumps your blood into tubes called blood vessels.

Blood vessels called arteries carry blood away from your heart to every part of your body. Blood vessels called veins bring blood back to your heart.

When you get hot, your skin may turn red. This is because blood rushes to the blood vessels in your skin to keep you cool.

Blood is constantly moving around your body. This movement is called circulation. It takes less than a minute for your heart to pump blood to every part of your body!

Activity

Hold your left hand in the air for a few moments. Hang your right hand down by your side. Now look at the colour of each hand.

It is harder for your heart to pump blood upwards, so your left hand looks pale because there is less blood in it. It is easy for blood to flow downwards, so your right hand is more red.

Blood

Your blood carries oxygen from your lungs, and goodness from your food, all around your body.

Your blood is full of tiny cells, that carry oxygen. These cells give your blood its red colour.

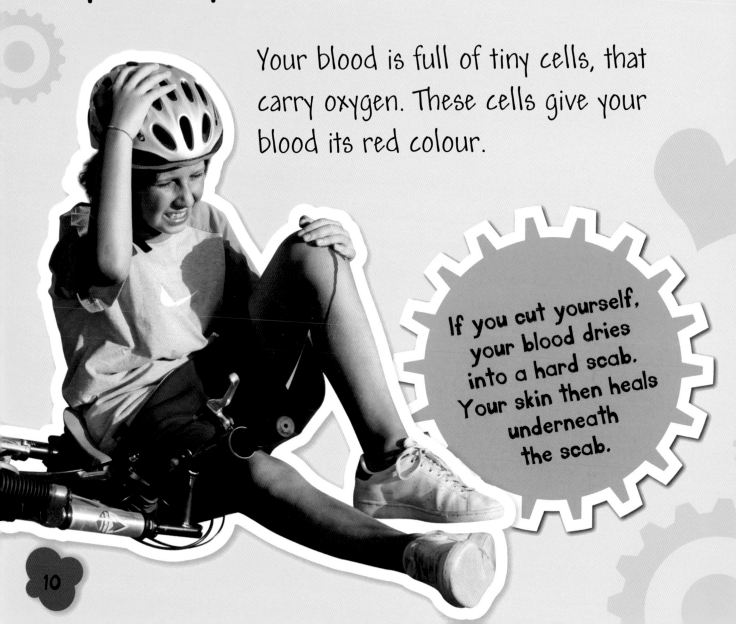

If you cut yourself, your blood dries into a hard scab. Your skin then heals underneath the scab.

When your body is working hard, if you are running for example, it needs more oxygen from your blood. This means your heart beats faster.

You can feel your heart beat by placing your fingers on the blood vessels on your wrists. This is called your pulse.

Activity

Feel your pulse. Now run on the spot for a few moments. Feel your pulse again.

Your heart usually beats about 90 times a minute.

Your pulse gets faster when you work hard.

Lungs

You use your lungs to **breathe** in air.
They are like two big balloons.

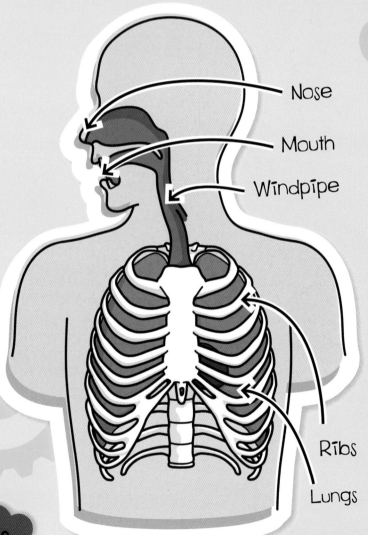

Nose

Mouth

Windpipe

Ribs

Lungs

To leave enough room for your heart, your left lung is a bit smaller than your right lung. Your lungs are protected by your ribs.

Your lungs are like sponges. They have lots of tiny bubbles which fill with air.

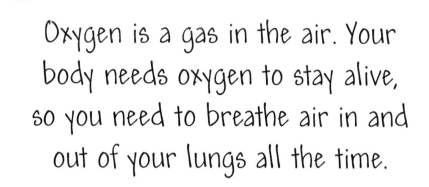

Oxygen is a gas in the air. Your body needs oxygen to stay alive, so you need to breathe air in and out of your lungs all the time.

▲ Humans can't breathe under water, unless they use a tube called a snorkel!

Breathe in...

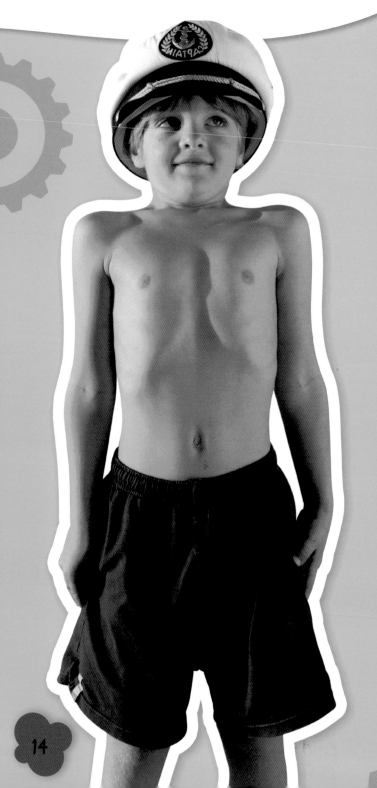

You use your mouth and nose to breathe in air. Air goes down your **windpipe** into your lungs and they get bigger as they fill up.

Tiny hairs in your nose and windpipe catch bits of dirt to make the air going into your lungs as clean as possible.

Oxygen from the air goes into tiny blood vessels in your lungs. Blood full of oxygen flows to your heart and your heart pumps it round your body.

Every day, the average person breathes in around 11,000 litres of air. That's enough to fill a whole swimming pool!

Breathe out...

After your lungs have taken oxygen from the air, you breathe out.

The stale air goes up your windpipe and out through your mouth and nose.

Activity

Put your hand near your mouth and breathe on it. Your breath feels warm.

The air you breathe out gets warm as it goes through your body.

When you breathe out on a cold day, you see the tiny drops of water in your breath like a cloud.

The air you breathe in is full of oxygen. The air you breathe out is full of a gas called carbon dioxide. Your body does not need carbon dioxide, so you get rid of it. Your breath also has tiny drops of water in it.

Sneezing gets rid of things your body doesn't want to breathe in. Fast!

17

Talking

You need your lungs to talk as well as to breathe. You speak and sing with a part of your windpipe called your voice box.

Activity

You can feel your voice box by gently touching the front of your neck. Make all kinds of different sounds – shout, screech and whisper. Does your voice box move when you make a sound?

You make sounds when air flows over folds of muscle called 'vocal cords' in your voice box. The more air that goes over the folds, the louder the sounds!

▸ Shouting uses lots of air. When you shout, you soon get out of breath.

Hiccupping is when air rushes in and hits your voice box.

Healthy heart and lungs

You need to look after your heart and lungs. Keeping active makes your heart and lungs work harder and this helps to keep your whole body strong and healthy.

Healthy eating

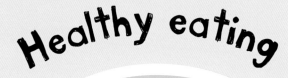

You can protect your heart and lungs by eating fresh food, lots of fruit and vegetables and not too much fat, salt or sugar.

Healthy food is good for you and delicious too!

Fresh air

Fresh air is good for your lungs. Sometimes the air in big cities is polluted by fumes from cars. Polluted air contains tiny bits of smoke and dust that enter your lungs and make you cough.

▲ Air is cleaner in the countryside and at the seaside.

Sleep

When you sleep, your brain keeps you breathing without you having to think about it.

When you wake up after a good night's sleep, you are rested and ready to start the day.

21

GLOSSARY

Blood
Blood is red liquid that runs through your blood vessels to every part of your body. It carries goodness from your food and oxygen from your lungs.

Blood vessels
Blood vessels are tubes that carry your blood. Arteries are blood vessels that carry blood away from your heart. Veins are blood vessels that carry blood back to your heart.

Breathe
You breathe air in and out of your lungs all the time. You breathe through your nose and mouth.

Muscle
Your muscles pull your bones so you can move. Muscles keep your heart beating and your lungs breathing.

Lungs
Lungs are the part of your body you breathe with. They take oxygen from the air and pass it to your blood.

Oxygen
Oxygen is a gas in the air. Your lungs take oxygen from the air when you breathe in. Your blood carries oxygen from your lungs all round your body. Every part of your body needs oxygen to stay alive.

Pump
A pump pushes liquid along. Your heart is a pump that pushes blood through your blood vessels.

Windpipe
Your windpipe is the tube that carries air into your lungs when you breathe in, and carries it out again when you breathe out.

INDEX

arteries 8

blood 4, 5, 6, 7, 8, 9, 10, 11, 15
blood vessels 6, 8, 11, 15
breathing 12, 13, 14, 16, 17, 21

capillaries 15
carbon dioxide 17
cells 10
circulation 9

exercise 8, 11, 15, 20

healing 10
heart 4, 5, 6, 7, 8, 9, 11, 15, 20
heart beat 6, 11
heart muscle 4, 6
hiccupping 19

lungs 12, 13, 14, 15, 16, 20, 21

mouth 12, 14, 16
muscles 4, 6, 19

nose 12, 14, 16

oxygen 7, 10, 11, 13, 15, 16, 17

pulse 11

ribs 12

scabs 10
skin 5, 8, 10
sleep 5, 21
sneezing 17
sounds 18, 19

talking 18–19

veins 8
voice box 18, 19

water 6, 13, 17
windpipe 12, 14, 16, 18

NEXT STEPS

❊ Show the children the position of your heart, just to the left and middle of your chest. Make a fist to show the size of your heart. An adult's fist is bigger than a child's fist. Talk about the comparative size of a child's heart and an adult's heart.

❊ Feel your ribs and breastbone. Discuss how your ribs protect your heart. Explain that your heart needs to be protected because it is soft. Use the word 'muscle' and ask the children to point out other muscles that let them move. Use the word 'pump' and talk about how a pump pushes liquid.

❊ Talk about how blood travels through blood vessels in the same way that water travels through pipes. Ask the children to find pipes around the home.

❊ Feel each other's pulse and explain that each beat is your heart pumping blood all round your body.

❊ Breathe in and out through your nose and mouth. Try putting your hand in front of your face. Feel air coming out of your nose. Now feel it coming out of your mouth. Ask the children if they think air comes out of both their nose and their mouth at the same time.

❊ Run together on the spot and feel how your heart beats faster and you breathe more quickly after exercise. Explain that this is because your body needs more oxygen when you work hard. Feel your heart beat and ask the children what they notice about their breathing when they rest.